D1642904

WITHDRAWN

DEMOLITION

A Spillage of Mercury
Spanish Fly

DEMOLITION

Neil Rollinson

CAPE POETRY

Published by Jonathan Cape 2007

2 4 6 8 10 9 7 5 3

First published in Great Britain in 2007 by
Jonathan Cape
Random House, 20 Vauxhall Bridge Road, London SW1V 2SA

www.randomhouse.co.uk

Addresses for companies within the Random House Group Limited can be found at:
www.randomhouse.co.uk

The Random House Group Limited Reg. No. 954009

A CIP catalogue record for this book is available from the British Library

ISBN 9780224081719

The Random House Group Limited supports The Forest Stewardship Council
(FSC®), the leading international forest certification organisation. Our books
carrying the FSC label are printed on FSC® certified paper. FSC is the only
forest certification scheme endorsed by the leading environmental organisations,
including Greenpeace. Our paper procurement policy can be found at
www.randomhouse.co.uk/environment

Typeset by Palimpsest Book Production Limited,
Falkirk, Stirlingshire
Printed and bound in the UK by
MPG Books Ltd, Bodmin, Cornwall

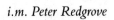

i.m. Peter Redgrove

Love is not the last room; there are others after it, the whole length of the corridor that has no end.

Yehuda Amichai

CONTENTS

ACKNOWLEDGEMENTS

Acknowledgments are due to the editors of the following:

A Winter Garland (Wordsworth Trust), *London Review of Books*, *The North*, *Poetry on a Plate* (Poetry Society), *Poetry Review*, *Rialto*, *Smiths Knoll*, *Tall Lighthouse Poetry Review*.

'Wildlife' was commended in the 2004 National Poetry Competition.

The epigraph by Yehuda Amichai is from his poem, 'Near the Wall of a House', taken from the *Selected Poems*, edited and translated by Chana Bloch and Stephen Mitchell (University of California Press).

Many thanks to the Wordsworth Trust, especially to Pamela Woof and David Wilson. Thank also to the Society of Authors for a Cholmondeley Award, the Arts Council for a Writer's Award, and the R.L.F. for a Writing Fellowship.

Special thanks are due to Robin Robertson, Louise Clarke, Michael Bayley, Henry Shukman, Paul Farley, Jacob Polley, Sarah Hall and Paul Beasley, to name just a few. And last, but not least, a huge thank you to all the mad folks of Grasmere. It was a great two years!

DEMOLITION

WILDLIFE

You get addicted to the ink,
or the pain; one or the other.
When she came in here for that rose

on her shoulder, I might've known
it would come to this – years later,
her body painted from head

to foot in a thousand colours.
I read her now like a picture book,
a china vase, a dream of my own making.

I've pierced her ears, her nose,
put studs in her nipples,
a silver ring through the hood

of her clitoris. I've covered
her breasts with moths,
her thighs with dolphins.

Her back is a forest of shrubs
and birds, her arms are vines,
her belly a nest of vipers.

I've touched her where only
a lover should touch, have heard her sigh
in the cold November dusk

of my studio. I've felt her burn,
at the brush of a finger, and hardly
a word passed between us.

I think of her sometimes lying
in bed, the buzz of my needle
still in her skin, a lover

tracing the braille of a new tattoo,
or him holding her, gently,
amazed at the wildlife swarming

under his hands, how she moves
in the flicker of candles; or watching
her sleep, how he loses himself

in the richness and distance.
The journeys he takes.
The stories he finds in her skin.

BELT

I'm on my knees, busy at her belt,
releasing the leather
from the buckle's spike,
popping it free from its hole,
she slides the full length of it
out with a flourish.
The jeans relax on her hips.
I watch the ring in her navel
rise and fall as she breathes.
There is only a stud and a zipper now.
I could take these off with my teeth.
But I'm on my knees before her,
feeling the loop of her belt
around my neck, the cold brass buckle
tight against my throat.

DEMOLITION

We can drop this building into a biscuit tin,
all forty storeys, everything's planned,
down to the last inch: the pre-repairs,
the pattern of charges:
nitro-glycerine, dynamite, RDX.

We study it for days,
from high ground or the tops of other buildings,
sorting our delay paths,
checking sequences from other jobs.
It's an intuition. A sixth sense.
We take the whole thing down in our heads.

Then we begin:
control the velocity of failure,
let each part of the structure disintegrate
at a different speed – we can make it
walk down the road, like a zombie.
We can turn it around, drop it ten floors
then stop it, dead; waltz it out of a corner
then lay it down in the road,
like a golem tired of standing.

After it's done, we check the debris,
the fragmentation pattern, see how
neat we've been. This is downtown Baltimore
and you can't move for skyscrapers,
cars, pedestrians. There isn't a scar,
a stone out of place, hardly a stir of dust
and the birds are singing. It's like nothing
was there: like nothing had happened.

CAULIFLOWER

Cut the crown from its stem
and settle it on the chopping board
like a hairdresser settles a head.
Take out the knife and cut through the crown:
a brain laid open, two halves
on the table-top, empty of thought,
a memory of rain and root, the bright
glance of a garden fork, perhaps,
and a star in the dark sky.

Ugly they might be; cabbages of sorts.
I carry them home like trophies:
the heads of Alfredo Garcia,
John the Baptist and Marie Antoinette,
dead weights in a Sainsbury bag.
Or look at it this way: a storm cloud,
a cumulonimbus of buttery florets
billowing up off the kitchen table.

What else can we do with this creamy wart,
this rough and bulbous monster,
its head full of dreams? Cook it, I guess,
in a curry with spinach and mustard,
bake in a strong cheese sauce,
or fry to a crisp tempura, seasoned
with sesame seed and a splash of soy.
Or how about ice cream? Blend it
with sugar, eggs and a jug of crème fraiche,
then serve on a medley of autumn fruits:
it'll still seduce with its deep and savoury edge,
that hint of horseradish under its breath.

H.M.S. VANGUARD V. LUIGI'S PIZZERIA

The first mention of cricket in Italy was of a match played by Admiral Nelson's sailors in Naples in 1793.

Luigi's leg spin is almost unplayable
as he lopes in from the Harbour end; Giovanni,
keeper of the *little wooden castle*

crouches behind him, Pedro, Bruno and Gino
on their haunches around the stumps.
Hardy is tied up in knots: flashing and flailing,

like his bat's made out of pasta.
Luigi lets one fly, Hardy can hear the seam
fizz as it spins through the air; all he can smell

is marjoram, basil and oregano.
He can think of nothing but food. After nine months
at sea, on a diet of barley and dried beef

this is Paradise: trees full of pomegranates,
almonds and persimmons; there are grapes on the vine,
the aroma of garlic roasting in ovens.

He watches the ball come out of the hand, trying
to judge the spin, but all he can see is pizza
smothered in olives, tomatoes and artichokes.

The ball pitches at leg. He's swatting at flies
as it turns inside and finds the gap. The bails
somersault onto the grass. Howeeezazat!

Luigi is wheeling away like an eagle,
arms outstretched, his waiters chasing him round the
    ground.
Hardy spits and wipes the sweat from his brow,

he drags himself back to the clubhouse, his throat
parched and his belly aching, picks up his wallet
and heads through the teeming streets to Luigi's

for a glass of beer, one of his finest pizzas
and a glance at his beautiful, dark-eyed daughter
who served him last night with more than a smile.

COLD

It's barely a sniff,
a scent on the breeze,
but it knocks me back thirty years
to a school corridor, to cloakrooms
where all the damp duffel coats hang
like pelts, the smell
of a gerbil cage, piss and liniment,
and the lips of a girl
whose face is a blur now,
and whose name is gone.
The boy too, he is no more me
than anyone else,
every cell in my body is new,
and she, if she were here
would say she never knew me.
But that smell is like yesterday
hard-wired into memory
and the touch too, her lips
still cold after all these years.

HUBRIS

Desperate for this girl
from fifth form,
for the touch of her body,
I stand in the garden
beside her,
full of myself,
exclaiming how
I hate my father
just as he opens the door
and steps outside,
and though I'm sure
he could never
have heard what I said,
I'm troubled
by an uncharacteristic smile,
boy-like yet full
of worldly suffering
as he nods his head
at the two of us
and wanders through.

KISS

Blood-red lipstick,
her mouth open like a cut.
I want to feel its heat
on my lips, on the tip
of my tongue.
I watch a cold rosé,
coral-pink, pass her lips
and I want to be wine.
She takes a cigarette
and I yearn to be smoke,
sweet and gun-metal blue
entering her through
bronchiole and alveoli.
With a mouth like that
she can suck the soul clean
out of my body,
taste me, roll me around
on her tongue,
then put me back
with a single kiss.

NIGHT WATCH

Grandad would stay awake all night
in those last days, hoping to catch death
on its way through the cold house,
to see it face to face, eyeball
to eyeball, and stare the thing down.

I hold his old Timex, the strap cracked
and weathered, the face still vaguely
luminous in this gloomy room;
the still hands pointing west,
eight forty-five some bleak morning
or evening, before I was born.

My father sits beside the fire now
rocking his chair, watching the clock
on the mantelpiece. He can see
the hour hand moving, he tells me
in his brighter moments; how time
speeds up, the closer you get.

On watch, he says. Like his father.
Soldier's talk. Then he's fast asleep
under the lamp: a sitting duck.

PRELUDE FOR POPCORN, COUGH, AND MOBILE PHONE

It begins like this: in silence,
then out of the calm, a pizzicato
of cello; a clarinet, then high above,
a single oboe sings, contemplative, dark
and rich in mystery – so it comes as a shock:
the first rustle of a Quality Street,
the purple kind, like a shower of rain
drenching a lawn: a stifled cough,
distant, pathetic, an old man perhaps,
caught in the downpour.
Here the famous leitmotif is introduced:
the trill of a mobile phone, sudden,
stunning; like birdsong after the storm.
The middle section develops the theme –
an improvisation of everyday items:
popcorn, pagers, keys and coins,
a controversial, post-modern masterpiece,
brilliant in its bare-faced cheek.
The critics are scathing but the punters love it.
For the coda, the music settles, a cello moans
and wrings the last heartbreak
out of the night, supported by yawns,
stretching, a distant chorus of snores.

WORLD SERVICE

Even now, in the hot sun
with a Piña Colada,
at five o'clock GMT
I bend to the radio,
searching for the BBC
World Service, and Sports Report:
the steady, hallowed tones of
James Alexander Gordon
reading the football results.

That litany of place names,
a hymn to mist and darkness,
from Plymouth to Inverness,
a whole country under rain,
the stadium lights flooding
the sky, that brief blue glimpse
of summer above the towns.

This voice, calm, unwavering,
has talked me through un-numbered
tea times, in steamy kitchens,
dad marking the pools coupon
with a steady pencil stroke,
hoping for those eight score draws
that always eluded us.

It almost seems exotic
sitting here now, travelling
through all the damp corners
of Britain, still listening
for the crucial result:
Newcastle one, Sunderland nil,
or that fabled Scottish score
of East Fife four, Forfar five.

ONIONS

It's enough to bring tears to your eyes
this talk of a modified onion, tamed
and impotent, shorn of its magic properties,
the power to make you weep over chutney,
to blub like a baby while making salad or salsa.
You've sharpened your knives and chopped
in goggles, you've vinegared your board,
you've soaked the bulbs, but nothing has helped.

Sacred symbol of the universe,
cure for baldness, dog bites and warts,
steroid for Roman Olympians,
enemy to aphid, weevil and carrot fly,
polish for copper and glass.

White Spear, Tokyo Long, Beltsville Bunching,
Walla Walla, Rossa Lunga di Firenza,
Red Globe, Ebenezer: drying in sheds all winter.

They've been diced in the houses
of ancient Egypt, Greece, and Mesopotamia,
whose cooks have sobbed in their sculleries,
cursing the spirits who live in the kitchen ceiling.
They wept on the Mayflower taking them overseas,
and the Queen of Hearts demanded the head
of the one who brought turnips instead.

So slice it with reverence, cut the green flesh
and watch it bleed. Feel the burn as you take it apart,
this papery ordance full of tear-gas and milky sap.
Lay down your knife and grip the table, rock
on your heels, like a god full of human suffering,
dream of your supper, and weep.

FORECAST

When I need a weather forecast,
I ask my grocer. Who else knows more
about rain or shine, of how the day will pass,
whether in sadness or hope.
The ache in his bones speaks to him,
as the apples and heads of celery whisper
their forecasts, their arcane vegetable knowledge,
to this man who works the pavement in a long
brown coat. His tables are stacked
with artichokes, grapefruit and garlic,
he communes with asparagus and avocados,
the rusty blush of oranges
the crispiness of lettuce.
He can tell by the crunch of a russet
how autumn will end, he knows
by the sweetness of plums, how deep
the snow will lie this winter.
His carrots are waxy, his mushrooms
plump in their balsa wood trays.
He rubs his hands, releasing the scent
of fennel and thyme. He gives me a pear,
and tells me to listen – not with my ears,
but my tongue, to taste what it says.
I measure its weight and texture. I take a bite,
and offer him clear blue skies, unbroken sunshine,
he grins like a sphinx who knows
only the language of fruit and veg.
His lemons dream of Granada, he says,
his cocoa of Lima, his bananas of Pushkar.
Shut out the noise in your head, the apples
are speaking, the goosegogs are chanting,
and look, the first spots of rain are beginning
to fall, he says, can't you hear, the tangerines
have been warning of this all morning.

BORGES: SUICIDE

Not a star will be left,
not even the night will survive.
When I croak, the whole
intolerable lot will disappear.
I'll erase pyramids,
gold and silver,
continents and faces.
I'll scrub the past,
make dust of time,
dust out of dust.
I can see the last sunset,
hear the last bird-song.
I'll take everything.
I'll leave nothing to anyone.

NERUDA: ODE TO AN ATOM

Tiniest
star,
you seemed
forever
locked
in metal,
your devouring
fire
hidden away.
One day
they knocked
on your minuscule
door.
It was man.
With one
big bang
he unchained you
you saw the world
and came
into daylight,
you travelled through
cities,
your brilliance came
to light up our lives,
you were
a terrible fruit
of electric beauty,
you came
to hurry the flames
of summer,
and then,
with a tiger's lenses,
dressed in armour

and a chequered shirt,
wearing sulphuric moustaches,
and a porcupine's tail,
the warmonger came
and seduced you:
sleep,
he told you,
curl up,
little atom,
you are like
a Greek God,
a springtime
couturier of Paris,
sleep on my fingernail,
lie in this little box,
and then
the warmonger
popped you in his pocket
as if you were simply
a Yankee pill,
he travelled the world
and dropped you
on Hiroshima.

We woke up.

The dawn
had been consumed.
All the birds
had fallen like ash.
The smell
of graves
and tomb gas
roared through space.
The head

of the punishing
superman
rose, horrendous,
a bloody mushroom,
cupola,
cloud of smoke,
sword
of hell.
The burning air rose
and death spread
in parallel waves
reaching
the mother asleep
with her child,
fish
and fishermen,
bakers
and their loaves,
the engineer
and his buildings;
all
was a blistering dust
a murdering air.

The city
crumbled,
and fell,
fell suddenly,
demolished,
rotten,
men
were lepers,
they took
the hands
of their children,

and the tiny
hands came off
at the wrists.
And so,
from your hiding place,
the secret
stone mantel
in which the fire slept
they took you,
furious spark,
scorching light,
to destroy life,
to pursue
the distant creatures
under the sea,
in the air,
on the beaches
in the last
corners of the ports,
to erase
the seeds,
to murder the cells
and stunt the flowers;
atom,
they had you
demolish
nations,
turn love to a black scab,
burn our piled up hearts,
annihilate the blood.

Crazy spark,
return
to your shroud,
bury yourself

in those mineral cloaks,
return to the blind stone,
forget the warmongers,
collaborate
with life, growth,
supplant the motor,
elevate your energy,
fertilise the planets.
Now
you have no secrets
walk
among men,
without your terrible
mask,
setting the pace,
and speeding
the passage of the fruit,
separating
mountains,
straightening rivers;
making fertile,
atom,
overflowing
cosmic
cup,
return
to the peace of the vine,
the velocity of joy
to the embrace
of nature,
work alongside us
and instead of the deathly
ashes
of your mask,
the unleashing hell

of your anger,
instead of the menace
of your terrible light,
give us
your awesome
rebelliousness
for our grain,
your unbridled magnetism
to bring peace among men,
so it won't be hell
your blinding light,
but happiness,
morning hope,
your earthly contribution.

FORMAT C

You'd think it had a mind of its own
the way it behaves: wilful, vindictive,
plotting all night as I sleep,
waiting for me to open my latest creation,
then crashing the whole shebang,
mid-sentence, before I can save.
Well, I can be a vicious bastard too.
Remember the scene in *2001*
where Dave pulls the plug on HAL,
and all the while it's singing
that sad little song. *Daisy, Daisy* . . .
It broke my heart the first time round,
but now – older, wiser – I understand
the cold satisfaction of turning it off.

I mutter the mantra, the magic word
that will put it to sleep, forever.
I type the letters slowly, gleefully:
F.O.R.M.A.T. which means death, then C
which means him, her, it, whatever pronoun
it goes under, then all that is left to do
is press Enter which means the end,
the dark night of the silicon soul, cyber oblivion.
I hit the key and the world is freed of another tyrant.
I feel cleansed, exhilarated, powerful.
Now I will build a new regime, an installation
in my own image, clean and efficient.
The computer is dead, long live the computer.

AWAY WITH THE MIXER

Now there's no mind left,
since he can't remember his own flesh and blood
for more than an hour or two,
I think of my own forgetfulness:
simple things, like did I lock the door?

★

There's a call from the nurse:
he's out again, escaped the home,
the wily old bastard, off to Pudsey
to visit his sister. They drive him back
in an ambulance, his face smashed up.

What the fuck are you up to Dad,
she's been dead ten years.
But this is all news to him.
Dead? Georgina?

He wants to visit his Mum and Dad:
what can you say?
We told him last night, we're telling him now,
we'll tell him again tomorrow.

★

It's written in genes, copies itself
over and over, through generations,
that's what I'm thinking: it's in the family.
Granny was off with the show-folk,
mad as a bat. I remember her now
cackling away in the back of the Hillman.

It's either this, or the ticker – or cancer.
Maybe it's best to slip into mindless fog,
beyond caring, to be dead already.

★

Where did I park the car, he says.
You came in an ambulance, Dad.
Remember the ambulance?
He stares from the hospital window
into the car park, the fading light,
looking for a car he drove in the 1960s.

★

He's moved into somewhere secure,
with locks on the door,
but he gets through the kitchen
into the cemetery, cracks his head,
and this time it's the terminal ward.

★

We sit round a bed in which all
who have slept have died.
This was not where Lazarus lay.
He's wired in, hates the oxygen mask,
the pipe up his cock.

It's all body now, the proteins going,
his brain turning to sponge.

He sweeps the hair from his eyes,
an unconscious gesture,
not the sexual flourish it used to be;
that casual flick of the wrist.
Always a ladies' man, they tell me.

★

It's embarrassing being here,
but who admits to that?
The doctor arrives with a smile,
asking if we'd like them to
'intervene' in the 'event of . . .'
and I'm thinking, what the fuck for.
I'd pull the plug now if I could;
that's what he's muttering
under the mask, the morphine.
Can't they hear?

I should ask about the complications:
the virus he caught in here,
the pneumonia that's finally twisting the knife.

The nurse is full of smiles, bubbly,
barely out of her teens. I watch her arse
up and down the corridor, dreaming
of somewhere else, something else.
What draws her to a place like this?
What does she think about
as she drains his chest, wipes his mouth
and tucks him up, just as she did
for the last man who died here?

*

He opens his eyes, but there's nothing there,
no focus – like he's looking beyond us,
into his own place, watching the last things fade:
the face of a mother, a dusty kerb
in the twenties, marbles and wooden spinning tops.

These are not the windows on the soul,
unless the soul has bolted, and all you see
are the holes it's left. The chest rattles,
the body coughs up – this is the separation
they talk about, that old Cartesian chestnut,
clear as daylight: two separate things.

*

It's half three in the morning
when I get the text, that rotten time
of day when the grip is tenuous,
when the nearly-dead let go.

Mid-winter, the whole country under snow.
Better than slipping away at the height of summer;
the pre-dawn light in the curtains,
your ears full of birdsong.

*

They shoulder him in
past all the empty pews,
Allegri's *Miserere*
pours through a hi-fi
and, briefly, I'm moved;
I feel rinsed through, breathless,
full of unlikely grief.

At the Chapel of Rest
we have Glenn Miller's *In The Mood*,
closing proceedings:
three minutes and eighteen seconds
of dance music as the body of the old man
heads for the kiln. I look at the preacher
and the preacher looks at me, and I turn
to look at the ceiling beams.

Peter Sellers started this nonsense –
of course the track gets stuck, and somebody
makes a dash for the CD player;
it's laughs all round as we head for the door
and the winter sunshine, glad it's over,
that these things are only committed once.

★

The sun sets on the Pennines,
the arse-end of Bradford – barely four
and dark already. The smell of moss
and leaf mulch fills the Garden of Rest.
I piss on a rhododendron, and think:
I'm shot of this now, the family thing.

★

The ring-road motel is not a place
of contemplation, its utilitarian comforts
more suited to stag do's, and swingers' nights.
I stand at the window watching the houselights
shiver in darkness, all the town spread out;
this is the place I was born, where he was born,
his father before him. Now he's gone
I won't be back, it's like goodbye
to geography, to the limestone county
I hated and loved, where we all grew up.

I head for the restaurant, a steak
and a bottle of wine, alone at last.
I toast myself in the black windows:
tomorrow I'll be out of here, heading south.

★

Not much to show after eighty odd years:
a bagful of tools, a snapshot or two.
That could be me in his wedding photo:
spitting image. I look at the eyes, the hair,
the line of his jaw: like looking in a mirror.

★

I sit on the bus, running it through in my head:
back door, windows, gas ring.
I check my pockets for keys and wallet.

It's times like this he comes to me,
sat on a hospital bed, swinging his feet
like a child, packed and ready to leave,
that look in his eyes –
of bewilderment, or wonder.

GIFT

I stand in the dark garden and watch
as the neighbour's daughter, unclothed
and just sixteen, combs her long red hair.
I stand there open-mouthed at this
sudden gift, every inch of her a miracle
of naked beauty, she smiles and combs,
and looks right at me, unabashed, except
she can't see me at all, and is only looking
at her own reflection in the glass.
I'm snared, a creature mesmerized
by the cobra's gaze. I daren't move
or even look away in case she sees me
standing here, watching. She turns,
to see herself side-on: the shape of her breasts,
her belly, the curve of her arse, then turns
to me again, her arms wide open, grips
the curtains and pulls them shut. A chill
runs through me, like Actaeon must have felt
in the woods. I hear the dogs bark in the suburbs,
the way they bark when something dies,
or is lost, like youth, or love, or innocence.

BORGES: THE MIRROR

As a child I feared the mirror
would show me another face,
a blind, inhuman mask that hid
something hideous. I feared also
that the silent time of the mirror
changed the course of the hours of men,
and kept in its vague, imaginary space,
new beings and forms and colours.
(Being a timid child
I spoke of this to nobody.)
Now I fear the mirror holds
the true face of my soul, injured
by shadow and faults, the one
that God sees, and perhaps men too.

CUCUMBER

Eight inches of flesh and water,
thick as a cock in your fist,
the skin ribbed and rutted
for grip, and sensitivity.
Some like it peeled,
so the juice comes off in your hands,
a creamy lather, cool in the palm.
Some prefer the mooli,
with its human texture,
all mass and density: a serious root.
But this afternoon
only the cucumber fills you
with ripeness like this,
cold from the fridge,
the scent of summer filling your room.

ANIMA

I look in this mirror and find myself
transformed into a woman.
I study my new features,
the high cheekbones, the lips
full and plum-dark, the eyes brighter now,
smooth-cheeked, almost good-looking.
The difference a single chromosome makes.
I'm held by her gaze, that sadness
behind her eyes, as if she knows
my weakness and fears for me.
I stand in front of the glass and stare,
like the man on a station platform
watching the face of his lover
fade through a train window.
She stays all night, I can't get her out
of my head, that face, those eyes –
my other half, my twin sister, my anima,
whoever she is, or was, I know
I'll never touch her, or see her face again.

DOLL

He goes in fear of prams
and push-chairs, avoiding the mums
who gather in gangs outside the crêche.
The eyes of a doll seem deeper,
more full of misery than a saint's.
The modern ones are bearable,
with their plastic faces and puffy hands,
crying and pissing their nappies,
a string-pull between their shoulders.
But the old ones with their heavy,
porcelain heads – they stare beyond you
into your past. They have outlived
all their children, and he knows
when they open their eyes
they can see right through him.

WAITING FOR THE MAN

On the corner of Kawaramachi
and Teramachi-Dori
we're waiting for the man to change
from red to green.
We stand in the hot sun,
six of us in line,
like men waiting to be shot.
Some wear face-masks
others are dripping in suits and ties.
A girl pulls up on a bicycle,
her lacy parasol dark
with recent rain.

The street is empty; steam
eases itself off the wet road.
I drink from my bottle of Pocari Sweat.
The label informs me
*this refreshing drink has been
a long time favourite of many people.*

A geisha clip-clops to a halt on the kerb,
her red kimono full of birds;
on the other side, Ganguro girls
stand in perfect stillness.
We face each other over the road.

It's so humid I can feel the water
dance on the hairs in my nose.
Up on the hill the bamboo
sways like swords in a battle.

The street is empty and narrow
but it might as well be
the Kyoto–Tokyo Expressway,
a no-go area between war zones.

An aeroplane catches the sun,
flares for a moment, then disappears.
A woman sits in front of her apples,
her shadow painting the pavement.

Two men are playing mah-jong
while a record player
scratches Verdi from an old LP.

A calm envelops everything:
the old man who used to think
that Hirohito was a god,
the old woman who survived Kobe,
and still believes in ghosts.

You can hear the chink of porcelain
behind shut screens, the tap-tap
of chopsticks on lacquer-ware bowls.
Flags and paper lanterns hang in stillness.

Can't we just cross?
There's nothing coming
in either direction.

A man on a bicycle pedals by,
we've been expecting him for years.
He rings his bell as he passes.
And still we wait.
The whole of Japan is waiting
on the edge of the pavement,

the last of the pink cherry blossom
shivers, and will not let go.
The bamboo sways, like a million
blue pencil strokes, a gentle
cross-hatching over the hill.

★

As you slept last night,
I drank my Kirin beer:
Brewed for Good Times,
topping-up my glass
to the 'harmony line'.

I watched the city
from the hotel window,
the pools of blue light
from vending machines,
like phosphorescent creatures
glowing in a dark sea.

I stood and looked,
but the more I saw,
the less I could fathom.

★

This afternoon I sat in the garden
of Tenryu-ji Temple,
and fell asleep where Muso Kokushi,
the old priest, must have slept
a thousand years ago, one ear
on his ever expanding consciousness,
the other tuned to the turning world:
butterflies alighting on maple flowers,
rice growing plump in the paddy fields,

koi cruising the ornamental ponds,
a crane-fly walking on water.

I heard all these things as I slept,
and travelled far, this was the dead
centre; tuning fork for the world.
When I woke we were poised
on the edge of the kerb, still waiting
to cross the road.

★

Sweat rolls down my nose;
someone bows to somebody else;
another bike passes, its spokes shred the light
like a Catherine wheel.
I can feel the shiver of cold sashimi
melt on my tongue, the sweetness
of soy glutting my mouth.
If we have to, we will wait all day.
Fans are furled and unfurled,
the girls are cooling themselves
in unison; my shirt is dark with perspiration.
An iPod fires up; I can hear
its faint snigger behind me.

Nothing is coming but we do not cross.
We stand at the edge of darkness
and light, waiting, as everything slips
into stillness, the song of a fantail,
the scrape of a wok on a gas ring,
a child bouncing a rubber ball;
in everything contentment,
everywhere peace and eternity;

the man glows in his bubble of red glass,
mid–stride, held in the still moment
between one step and another,
like the photo of a galloping horse,
caught with all four feet off the ground,
floating.

CHAOS THEORY AT THE 4.20 HANDICAP CHASE AT HAYDOCK PARK

Nothing is certain, especially here;
but Danzig Flyer, the odds-on favourite,
and a shoo-in to boot, is the form horse,
a dead cert for the 4.20 at Haydock Park.
I'm lumping on, in confidence.

But this is all it takes: the simple flutter
of money, the sound of a wedge unfurling,
to bring about catastrophe. Say nothing
of butterflies and distant earthquakes, just see
how a powerful racehorse runs like a pig,
or falls at the last while ten lengths clear,
and a green tarpaulin's slid from the back of a van.

The simple movement of money, from pocket
to bookmaker, brings out the vet, the pistol,
the bullet rifling down a barrel,
bringing the dark to a late spring meeting,
blood on the grass, the empty wallet,
that dream of another day, another race,
of chasing your losses forever.

Let's stand at the winning post,
between butterfly wing and the furl of a fiver,
let's do this again and sit the race out,
your money safely in hand, and watch
as Danzig Flyer, the odds-on favourite
annihilates the field! If you tossed a coin,
it would land on its edge; still, nothing is lost.

The bookies chalk up their prices,
at 4–6, Summertime Blues is a nailed-on certainty.
You slip the notes from your pocket,
and somewhere, a window rattles, crockery
shifts in a cupboard, and down in the basement,
a bullet waits in its chamber.

BORGES: IMAGINING THE DEATH OF COLONEL FRANCISCO BORGES (1833–74)

I leave him on his horse,
in that twilight hour when he looked
for death – of all the hours of his life
this is the one that endures: victorious and bitter.
They stride up the field, the whiteness
of horse and poncho, while death
waits patiently in the rifles.
Sadly Francisco Borges enters the plain,
shrapnel is everywhere, the rattle of bullets,
but all he sees is the boundless pampas,
this is what he saw and heard
all his life, day after day, in battle.
I leave him there, in his epic universe
dignified, almost untouched by the verse.

TORNADO

It's here without warning, a sudden
shriek, and it's down your throat –
so low you can see the payload
slung below the wings, the pilot
nursing his joy. Too late – it's hit you –
the windows rattle their frames,
the *Moonlight Sonata* struggles for sense
as the radio judders along the window ledge.
The sheep in the field continue
their slow munching through grass,
oblivious, they've seen it all before.
It turns with a rumble: beautiful
the way the air holds it, how it weeps
in the atmosphere, the watery vortices
trailing off wingtips; it throttles out
and is gone, a dot on the far horizon.
Immaculate. How can you not love it?
The whole valley could be ash by now
and we'd never have felt a thing.

GPS

The dark comes quickly here, like doubt,
at four the colour drains out of everything;
fog stirs on the hill and the path dissolves.

High Raise: bitch of a fell in winter,
gloomy and dank, silent, except for the tick-
ticking of moss as it drinks. You walk

by your nerves, the map redundant as you sink
into darkness and panic. Thank God
for your GPS, its ghostly glow in your hand,

for satellites hung above you, cold, angelic,
guardians to lost hikers, fools and the reckless.
They plot your route step by step.

You pray for the life of your batteries, and trust
in a science born out of war, and slaughter.
You follow blindly, letting them guide you down,

as they guide a missile down the air-con shaft
of a factory where the innocent crouch.
You move through a valley, bog after bog,

then over the lip of a ridge, stony and buckled,
walking from waypoint by waypoint,
into a gentler landscape, the sound of sheep,

a beck somewhere, crashing the stillness,
a dry stone wall, miracle of the sudden path.
The lights of a distant farm blister the darkness

and you're down, buzzing, walking on air
all the way to the pub, where you toast
your little beauty with a pint, a kiss and a prayer

to providence, to missile systems brooding in silos,
to Euclid and Newton, to the intrigues of sine,
cosine, and tangent for getting you home.

BALLOONING

It clears the trees, the pin-sharp steeple,
the roofs and chimneys in London Road.
You can hear the hiss and groan as it
struggles for height. The other balloons
are up in the clear blue sky: top-hats,
bananas and polar bear, but the world's
biggest penis is holed and coming down.
We stand with our beers on the roadside,
watching it lurch and swerve, the pilot
fighting the droop above his head.
Passengers neck the Champagne
and grip the basket, their anxious voices
drift on the breeze. There's only
the postage stamp of a bowling green
for a landing. The burners ignite
in a last-ditch growl, and the gross shadow
of the Brobdingnagian member
fills the green, scattering pensioners
starting an end. He puts it down
with a bump, right on the crown, tipping
the squealing occupants onto the grass:
hampers, bottles and broken glasses.
A cheer goes up from the Hat and Feather
as the wasted envelope flops
on the floor like a giant's condom.
The other balloons are miles away,
riding the thermals, dots in the sky.

THE PATH OF A THOUSAND
HELLOS

'When all at once I saw a crowd'

It begins at the garden gate; by the time
you reach How Top you've greeted seven,
more by the pond and four by the stile,
their jolly rounded vowels mingling
with brook and crow, a thousand blended notes:
hello, hello. By White Moss Common
there's sixteen more: *good morning, hi,*
that mindless ramblers' bonhomie, as if,
because were out here, all together,
we ought to greet each other, heartily.

Give me Regent Street on Monday morning,
that sense of solitude you find in the city.
I can walk the mile of Oxford Street in perfect anonymity,
or stroll from Clerkenwell to Notting Hill
and never greet a soul though thousands pass,
it's like a journey through wastelands full of ghosts;
but this is hell, hailing everyone you meet,
the vapid smiles, the grins, the beaming faces.

At Rydal Mount there's half a coachful,
brimming with the bliss of Lakeland, poetry,
the romance of it all. *Hello, what a beautiful day.*
Like fuck it is, you want to say, but don't.

I leave the track and head up over Heron Pike,
the long, steep slog to Fairfield, where I know
that few, if any, will have ventured: the gnarled
and wizened, the grumpy or the antisocial;
this is where I like it, in the vicious gale, where words
get blown away before they're ever heard,
and a simple nod will do, to recognise a kindred soul,
out seeking solitude among the hills.

NATURE TABLE

First there were toadstools and acorns,
mistletoe, newts in a jam–jar,
innocent treasures of autumn;
then Henderson, the teacher's pet,
brought in the fossil of a fish
his father had found in a quarry.

The classroom was stunned; we studied
the fins and the delicate bones:
a cartoon comb etched in slate.
It was dinosaur fever all week long.

On Sunday night while mum and dad
were glued to the telly, I dug
through roses and gladioli
wondering what might be left
of Benji, our old Alsatian.
A pile of bones? Maggots
crawling on flesh? I'd heard
how your hair continued to grow
in the grave, your nails too.

When I found the skull
I couldn't believe its gruesome beauty,
the hairline cracks and hollow sockets,
the yellow teeth still in its jaw.
I kissed it. My muddy trophy,
bright in the light of the windows.
I rinsed it under the bath tap,
cleaned it up with a toothbrush.

At school, when I pulled the skull
from my duffel bag I heard gasps,
the whispers of admiration.
Was it a wolf? A coyote?
A tiger escaped from the zoo?

An Alsatian, said Henderson,
a badger, said Mrs Beal,
but no one believed what they said.
It sat there, inscrutable, mute
as a god in the classroom's hush,
while Henderson's fish disappeared
into somebody's duffel bag.

BULLFROG

The name's Bullfrog,
the amazing Mr Pumpkin-Head.
I'm a blower at the glassworks.
My cheeks are like bellows.
I can make whatever you want.
My creations are famous.
I can blow you the frailest of orchids
if that's what you'd like; a portrait,
a ball-gown in Vaseline glass,
goldfish in bowls of blue water.
A glass harmonica.
I turn sand into chandeliers
like magic, quartz into mirrors
and rose windows.
I have glass in my veins,
I sweat lime and soda-ash.
Half man, half milk-bottle,
as the wife liked to say.
I sleep in the foundry now;
the world outside is brown and lustreless.
I'm blowing a new head for myself,
a beautiful Millefiori job, and a bride
of the finest lead crystal:
so delicate, I'll need hands
of chamois just to touch her.

HONEY

They swarm over gardens,
a dark tornado, a maelstrom
of sooty particles searching for home,
the new queen somewhere
in its swirling centre,
then down the chimney:
a plume of smoke in reverse,
like coals in the hearth
sucking their dark heart
back to the source.
They mass beneath floorboards
building combs, making honey
inside the walls, you can hear the drone,
the buzz of insect life at dawn.
When you touch a wall it hums
like a drum, you can feel the tingle,
the far-away dull vibration
in the soles of your feet as you walk
barefoot from room to room.
It gathers all summer, toffee
and clover pollen filling the air
until the sweet scent of honey
drives you out of the house.

PÂTÉ

1

Taste a forkful my friend,
savour the texture,
geese have been tortured for this –
note how it melts in the mouth,
how the sweet scent of offal
fills up your head.

We're not talking carrots or turnips,
the innocent food of the macrobiotic,
but pâté. This is where blood and flesh
and transformation meet on the palate,
the taste of guilt and complicity
ripe on the tongue.

2

The vegetarians sit at the table
as if under a curse, pale and blameless,
knocking their clogs together,
discussing the merits of cabbage
and broccoli – which we also enjoy
as an adjunct to the brisket,
turning them over in a gravy of blood.

Give me a woman who likes her steak
bleu, her sweetbreads plump and proud
on the dinner plate, who takes her oysters
straight, and swallows in one go,
who likes her cheeses strong and veined;
a connoisseur of offals, and blood puddings.
A woman who likes her beef on the bone,
and swabs her plate with a chunk of bread.

3

The condemned man in his cell
knows after this last meal –
a ravioli of foie gras in truffle sauce,
and a glass of sweet white wine –
that he won't feel a thing
as the bullet enters his brain.
You can't kill a man who has feasted
in paradise. He's crossed the threshold,
he's home and dry, still at the table
mopping his mouth with a serviette,
ordering one more glass of cold Sauternes.

4

I fork this morsel into my mouth,
seared, flambéed in cognac and served
with a spoonful of rhubarb marmalade.
This is the swollen liver, the heart
of the issue, the nectar the French
have killed for, that Heliogabalus
fed to his dogs. Fuck
the duck, is what I think,
though in my heart I say a small prayer
for both of us. I take a forkful,
and another, until the plate gleams
and smiles back, a deep and satisfied grin.

BORGES: RAIN

It's raining now, clean and steady,
rinsing the afternoon. Or should I say
it *has* rained, since rain is one of those things
that happens in the past. Whoever hears

it fall will rediscover the time
when Lady Luck, being full of mischief
revealed to them, a flower called *rose*,
a bewildering redness of red.

This rain that blinds the glass, was happiest
falling in abandoned suburbs, among the black grapes
of vines in courtyards that no longer exist.

This drenched afternoon brings me the voice,
the voice I yearn for,
of my father, who's returned, and has not died.

∞

I look through this hole,
this tear in the cosmos,
and see how everything stirs

in the flux and swirl,
my life and yours.
I can see it all

swarm in the petri dish;
on this thin glass slide
beyond the lenses:

water, blood and cell.
I can hear your voice
moan in every molecule.

You can't split love
from an atom of carbon.
Look at the heart

of this nebula,
the incandescence
of birth and rebirth,

nova and supernova.
Notice how everything
tends towards iron,

even the diamond
set in your ring
how dull it is growing.

Look at the suns blink off,
one by one, the light
of the universe guttering out.

Give me a sum to describe
all this, an equation
to square this little circle.

Soon, my love, it will get
so cold a single thought
could finish us off.

VALLEJO: WAITING

Tonight I get down off my horse
and stand again at the door of the house
where I said goodbye that dawn.
It's shut, and no one answers.

The stone bench where mam
gave birth to my brother so he could
saddle the horses I'd ride
by street and fence, a village child,
this bench on which I left my painful
childhood yellowing in the sun;
its sadness frames the doorway now.

My horse sneezes, paws at the pavement
in doubt, this is his calling, the brute:
god in a foreign place. He sniffs,
neighs and shakes his clever ear.

Da will keep watch, praying,
and maybe he will think I'm late.
My sisters sing of their simple hopes,
beside themselves, preparing for the festival,
which is almost here. I wait, I wait,
my heart like an egg about to break.

It was a large family I left,
and not so long ago, but today
no one keeps watch, not even a light bulb
burns to welcome me home.

I call out, but there's no reply.
I stand there, weeping, and the animal
neighs, and neighs again.

All are sleeping now, forever,
and so deeply that my horse,
exhausted from shaking his head,
turns, half dreaming, and says to me
with every nod, that it's fine,
that everything is just fine.